REFLECTIONS WHILE LIVING IN UTAH

L. Flores

Cover & Art Design by Linda Lizbeth Flores
@lincpoetry
Edited by Alexis Rashak

For Kar, who always told me to write.

Table of Contents

REFLECTIONS WHILE LIVING IN UTAH

I.

Nights in Herriman

I'm standing in front of a 6 by 6 window
In a 6 to 7 figure home
Staring out at this small city's lights
Glittering
And sparkling,
Igniting sparks
In me.

The double pane window
So thick
The shine leads a glare to my eye,

And I want to be part of the cityscape.

Homes and street lights
Love stories evolving
And growing

Intertwining flutters of feelings all through the
Symmetrical numerical streets
Wet from the melted snow.

They hold hands along paved roads
Or sidewalks
Or in romantic alleys
Away from suburban norms—
High up the mountain side
I have the "best" view
The copper
Ivory
Green
Red
Yellow
Colors
Pulse.
Never sitting still
Like 21 year-olds downtown
Hopping from one event to the next
Entertaining themselves to death
With no regrets—
I want to be part of the cityscape.

Where there is drama
Unraveling

And unrequited admiration
Of acquaintances
And a girl is crying herself
To sleep
Because of cruel rejection's sting.

Where young friends go on
Platonic adventures
Through midnight
Streets

Prompting fate
To lead them
Away
Toward
An untold day
Or unanticipated feat
Or maybe
Even
A discovery

Of self,

Of connecting
Like roadways or one-way streets
That lead us all together
At
The
Center
…

Cars speed
Creating more
Colorful spatters.
The reflection of pools of Christmas green
And New Years' Red
Send
A rattle through
My spine
That clanks
And clatters
And tumbles down
Like spilling oil
Across the
Intersection,
And a pedestrian

Flicks his cigarette
And it all goes
Up
In
Flames.

…

I'll never
Be
Part
Of the
Cityscape.

Confined to beautiful four story homes
Nuclear families
And consistent tradition
(None of which are my own)
I'll grow old in
Their
Roots
And rules
And expectations
Of how to live a happy life—
Of how to please
Everyone
Else.

                    …

Because women
Have a great responsibility
And men have a solemn duty
To someone greater than themselves.
Because the greatest work you will do
Will
Be in that four story home.

I want to be part of…

Love Letter From my Space Heater to my Scented Candle
Modeled after Sarah Kay

I've been watching you
flicker
and fight.
I can tell your
energy is spent.

In a crowded room you are present
but your glow...
is dim.

The light
you provide
wears
thin.

I
admire
you
from
across
the
room
and
wonder
if you can feel the warmth
I'm sending you?

Do you feel
the
electricity
generating
kisses in
muffled white noises
all
along
your optimal
curves?

Do you feel
the
vibrations
below me

sending shivers
through the floorboards
up your glass face
through your cotton core?

There's a signal
atop my head
that illuminates the night
and messages you
like a lighthouse to a ship.

Did you find it?

In-between your cream colored skin
and charcoal covered eyelids
that flame like an iris
converts darkness into light.

Keep flickering
keep your fight
the
wick
is most
beautiful
when it's the
lowest
of the low;

When I'm cheering you on
to keep your glow;

do you feel the warmth
I
am sending you?
Your scent fills the room.
Do you feel
what I'm sending you?
Your light casts out the gloom.
Do you feel
what I'm sending you?
Your shadows bloom and dance across
the entire room.
Do you feel
what I'm sending you?

That spark

that flame
that heat
this game
messages I can't decode
and
I just have to know,
do you feel
the same?

From across the room,
do you notice me,
like I notice
you?

Do you feel the warmth I
am sending you?

…

As the night creeps on
my buzzing mind
wonders,
have I been wrong?

All this time
I'm watching you
burn
thinking at my
every
mechanical
turn
I might be the one
you
yearn
for.
Ridiculous!
I know.
Yet,
I cannot stop glancing
at your brilliant glow
your black roots
and yellow wave
beam
radiantly
into the night
and for a minuscule moment in time

I start to believe
you
not
only
feel my warmth…
but
I think
maybe…
possibly...

         …

              …

                    (impossibly)

You   feel   me.
You   know   me.

Because
we share this room.
Because we share similar
physical qualities
like
providing
heat.

I knew what you were the minute
our eyes met.
And
that's just a moment
you don't forget.

So, once more
Because I need to be sure.

In this
crowded
hollowed
room
that feels
like its filled
with just
me
and
just
you

Do you feel
the warmth
I am

desperately

sending
you?

Before

I am a Black Eyed Susan.
Surrounded
Isolated
Outlooking
A sea
Of possibilities—
Trapped
On a moutain side.
My neck
Stretched
Extended
Reaching

but planted firm

immovable.

Impersonating
Sunflowers—
But

I lament in the dark.

Within Yet Without

A peculiar feeling
To be calmed
By the soothing
Songs of crickets
In a master-planned community—
Much like the one I once wished
To escape as an adolescent.
Now, as an adult,
I seek out
The ducks
In man-made lakes
Carefully
Designed
To fit,
Precisely
Molded,
Aesthetically
Pleasing.

Not 25 feet from my beautifully crafted
Bench
Which outlooks the
Cattails—
A traditional
Family shoots photos,
Smiling with their three children,
Posing in a generically framed scene.

Irony.
All around me.

Surrounding myself with
Settings so
Normal Rockwell—
So
Ensign
Cover
Worthy,
So
Unlike
My childhood fantasies
Of what my life would be.

I imagined myself a city girl
With a loft apartment
And a wide window view of high rise
Buildings and gleaming electricity.
I imagined a girl there too—
Brick walls & bare ceiling
Enclosing us.
She was someone too beautiful to be with me.
Someone so clearly out of my league.
Or galaxy.
Or universe.
Someone who liked my poetry.
And I counted myself lucky to have even
Her glance.

Now
I watch the sunset
Behind the grey identical rooftops.
Behind the red iron bridge—
It stretches
Across Oquirrh Lake
And I am
Alone—

A Caucasian couple
Jogs across the
Perfectly winding path.

Humorous—
How
I
Find
Comfort
In what
I'll
Never
Have.

How masochistic
To find
Peace
In a temporary
Home.
To torture

Myself
Over
&
Over
Again—

Immersing
Myself
Within
Yet

      Without.

Opposites
Modeled after Octavio Paz

If you are the stillness in punctuation.
        I am the run-on sentence
If you are the timid sunrise
        I am the landslip slide crash spotlight
If you are honey strawberry elixir
        I am the monster poison
If you are autumn leaves coloring dreams
        I am winter's darkest sleep
If you are the botanical garden
        I am the driest western frontier
If you are the scent of peppermint
        I am without pheromones
If you are the last light switch flipping off
        I am a hundred angry crowds

        Imploring
        your
        stillness
        like

                a
                run-on sentence.

After

Suddenly everything is now new.
Unlike before.
She cradles me and pulls me into her—
Caressing my neck
Kissing my ears
With her flirtatious
Words.
Leading my hands
To all her closeted dreams

—My greatest fantasy—

Saying all I've wanted her to say,
Unreal in every way.

She allows me to undress her
With my questions.
I pour compliments
Down her mouth.

It's the first time
I know unity.

She invites me
To adventure;
I search for signs of hesitation,
Or fear,
Or possible regret,

Only to discover
An eagerness in her
Silhouette.

Then
I feel
Palpitations—
I suffocate in skin
Biting the summits of body.

It's the first time
I know satiation.

What have I begun?

Vacant Whole

I am the Willow Tree figure titled "heart and soul,"
both in love and hollowed out by a

                faith
                and
                love

                that do not

                match, fit, or flow.

I am the scent & glow of the
hot cacao candle in my room.
I am from humidity & flat plains; mosquito bites
and damned fire ants.
I am unrequited—distant smoke that rises like a body wanting to stay,
but
rejected by
the flame.
I am the Christmas tree catching on fire
that year I got two guitars—now we play it safe—extinguishing traditions.
I am drifting.
I am from late night
mariachi bands in front
by the pool.
I am the nine-year-old who asked for her room
to be rolled in blue and black
and had stars painted across her ceiling—they lit up my room, illuminated by a
black light.
I wrote that scene before *Superstore* did.
I am "hija si"
that's what my dad said to me
when I asked for my window to the sky.
"Tu eres muy especial."

I am the *Christus*—inviting & intimidating, at once
"fall at my feet,"
but
"call on my name,"

                not
                what you'd expect
                from stone...
I am H-Town—
tex-mex flavor—
my Aztec blood will soak you in terror;

slit you with obsidian;
suffocate your oxygen
and make war paint from your heart;

                         pulsing,

                                 pulsing,

                                          in my hand.

I am eating tamales from a sixty-year-old woman
in Sharpstown on the second floor—feasting
on memories of my father's generosity—
paying her in twenties,
sixty more than needed.
I am my father's unsparing acts—(and none of his sins)
I am Kay, Gibson, Choi—liberal acts of beauty in giving and giving
of themselves,
the way poets and people do.
I am a poet person.
I am that poet from
7th grade
&
that person who is in
                  love and hollowed out.

Like that Willow Tree figure, complete compilations

                of a vacant

                —whole.

II.

The Old Basilica of Our Lady Guadalupe
Modeled after Samantha Kerksiek

The graffiti highways of Mexico City propel us like a racing
bullet toward colorful corruption—
the target; a city who has been tagged over
their relics & religion; decimating sacred ground.

I walk on uneven stone which leads me to a sinking
hallowed graveyard and listen
to inches that carry me below the heaviness
of confessions and pardons.

She was here once,
The cathedral whispers, earnestly
wanting us to believe—but no one listens, no one remembers.

I walk on the marble green black webs;
the veins lead me to a sinking
history.

Faithless steps of apostasy weigh the temple down,
and silent snaps of their lenses burning
crucifixes and smashing chandeliers,
creating cries ringing from stain glass.

I watch the Holy House's Saint weep with loneliness
at the misguided attempts of tourists trying to know

a lost faith

Found only
by disciples who pilgrim in the crimson
blood of martyrs' past and for
still lips who praise her name.

Nobody Ever Taught Me How to Breathe Under Water

At five (maybe six)
My swim lessons consisted
Of the basics;
Floating
Puppy-dog paddle
Blowing air out using my nostrils.
As lessons advanced
So did the challenges—
Assessments, as us teachers like to call them—
"look for the pink rings, collect as many as you can before you need air"

But

"coach, we all need air...to survive"

It was then I realized the true objective:
To see how long I could go... without air.
To see if I could
Survive.

I always loved a good challenge.

As any good teacher will tell you—
The objective matters.
Without it,
You don't have any direction
Without it,
You're swimming into a wall.
"Collect the rings"
Obtain ten points
Graduate by 22
Travel the world
Masters by 25
Homeowner by 27
Advocate for the "forgotten and downtrodden"
Published before 30
"recognized intellectual ability"
Endowed in the temple, have four kids, two of them adopted, serve in a presidency, raise God-fearing children, never stop nurturing, pay for their missions, endure to the end, attend four weddings, GRANDKIDS! Great-photo-perfect-getaways! Serve them all!
Give up yourself,
Become
Like

GOD.

.....................but.................

What is God like?
Is he like the bubbles that bloom from my lips when my lungs exhale?
Is he the glisten of salt water, or the sting of solubles?
Is the chlorine that washes of clean like when we are baptized?
Immersed
Filtered out
Deadening
Disinfecting—
The sin.

At 24 I still do backstrokes through the wrinkles in the water
And hold my breath.
Playing a dead man's game of

        Salvation
or
        Suffocation

The pressure that builds up in my ear drum
Seals me to heaven
But binds me like a buyer's anchor
The deeper
I dive
The tighter it digs
I'm running out of time
I'm running out of time
That scene from *Hercules* flashes through my mind—
How far MUST I go

        to be saved.

—how many souls do I swim pass
And question...

How
Did
They
Live
Without
Air?
Or did they?
Did they have what was needed to survive?
Special skills
They didn't teach me
In all those life or death lessons?
I've collected the rings,
Neon blended pink
Lined up like a sleeve,
But I am looking around and I don't know how to breathe—
Gotta accomplish it all
Pokémon shit mentality
Gotta catch 'em all
Drowning in a YMCA
SEA
Of self-inflicted expectations
Alone in this assessment
Assessing how long I can go…   without air?

But nobody ever taught me… how to breathe

                    Underwater.

And if God wanted me to,

            Why didn't God give me gills?

First Degree

Sometimes I think of the flame,
The mark
I made
A punishment—
Brand—
The way
Orange
Crimson
Wrestled &
Crawled
Climbed
Above
Cobalt—
Pronounced
Pink
Upon dermis
First
Superficial
Degree
Disgust—
With my belly
Bulging
With
Regret worthy of
Pricked wrists &
Peeled back
Skin—
Oh—
Yes, I deserve this.
Don't dream of warm rooftop promises—
You couldn't keep.
Cry & choke
Down your flame
Rib cage so bare
Cry & choke
On that flame
Burrow it—
You
Deserve
This.

Somedays I Race the Sun I

We're both crouching—
Our finger tips
Grazing the road
—our track—
Bended knee
Balancing
Bracing
At the
go—

I press down
Hard
Propelling
My sense of self
(I am not really running)
I'm driving
Pushing
Right up
Flexor foot
At an obtuse
           Slope
The road
Unfurling

I peek
At the sun
To be sure I'm keeping up
He is up
Confidently fixed
Burning his calves
Graceful
Elegant

I don't take my eyes off him now
Now I want to be running His solar system
The map, Mountain View
I sing "Ribs" so loud
And shake
White knuckled
Against black leather
And think of the burning temperatures
How you blind me
I sing so ugly
Torso elevated

Leaning
        Leaping

A high jump now

Reeling through your summer streaks
In the dead of winter
Rolling cascade
Rumored heat
Can you make it good?
Can you make me feel less alone?

You're tiring now
Choking on your promises
Facades
Straight pointer fingers and brilliant form
Like coach taught
Like Morris' laugh
Holding her back
You're holding back
Letting me win?
Or tired
Of the game?

I pull forward
You're slowing
I look to stare
Oil pastel orange

                Saturate
                My
                Sight

I open my mouth to kiss you
Or maybe to curse your teasing
I want it back
        *I want you back

We've only raced a moment

When I realize I've won—I can't kiss you
        now.

You're completely gone.

Again.

(I knew this might happen)

Just. Friends.

I didn't like the taste of
      Your moving on—
          In my mouth,

When I was the one
      who caused the purge—
         handed
         you
             the
             bottle,
       yet took
       the

            hemlock.

Somedays I Race the Sun II

And,
I, insecure,
Review my actions
Was it good for you?
Did I exhilarate you,
The way you enthrall me?
Was your excellence
Supposed to hurt a little?
Excite me
Engage me
Exhaust me
En route
To your possibilities
Or paradise?

When I find a place to park, I watch you walk
Home over the Wasatch hedge. It's only polite.

You paint the sharp cuts of the mountain
Butterflies in my stomach, wings lilac
And I know it's just your shadow shutting
The front door on our run.

I contemplate your abrupt departure.

You left me white spots in my retinas,
A gift perhaps to remember you by.

A keepsake equivalent
In memory—
Passionate
As
A
Queer
Kiss
Or a
Drifting
Butterfly.

I can't help
But want it back
I want you back.

                    Make me feel alive.

Mine of my Mind

I carry my stress in my shoulders
Some people carry theirs in ulcers.
Others it's in their eyes
Sunken—
Dried.

Lately I've been wondering what it means
To be alive.
What does it mean to
Kiss the earth
Without saying goodbye?
Or to admire a mountain's
Body
Without
Blowing a mine?

Women Attempt More but Men are More Successful

In conversation he told me,
"More poets commit suicide than any other type of artist."
That's what he heard from a podcast at least.
A type.
That my SAD
Combined
With
My
Expressions
Of self
&
Truth
Make me more likely
To go
Home—
A
Place
Only
Known
To my veiled
Memory.

What would it be like
There?
To have a
Peace of
God:
A saint's stillness:
A comforter's
Calm:
...
A type
More likely to
Park on the
Edge of
Autumn Lane
In the dead of
November—
Let the gas
Encroach
Upon my bronchi,
Envelop
My hope/lungs.

More likely
To soar off
Mountain View
In a rage
Arguing
With God
And finishing,
No,
Winning
With
A single move:
My demise.
More likely to feel at home
Through candy apple light
Inside the poison.
Leaping from physical planes
To spiritual ones.

Would I be happy?
Would I feel
Hope?

III.

Inner Space Cavern, Georgetown TX

Scalloped ceilings
In a cavern cathedral
Reflect
Crashing
Waves—
Literally
Trapped—
For possible decades—
Flooding
A sanctuary.
She sinks
Back to earth
Returning home.
　　　　It is done.

But

Crescent curves
Are the residue,
Marking
The times I flooded my faith with fear—
When I let "queer" thrash my back

Let it carve
Broken
Let it carve
Wrong

　　　…

Let it carve

Healing
Let it carve

Whole.

Suddenly a place submerged
In agony
Emerges
Into my place of refuge,
Tear-dropped-developed cones
Are waxed candles
And alters
And baptismal pools—
I kneel
And the echoes of God's tears drip on my face;
Icy cold—
But clean.

I am clean.

In this house of worship
Ghost waves surround me
Reminders of the blood.
Ghost insults surround me
Reminders of the flood.
I look up
Seeking
Punishment
For
Sin

But
All
I see
Is
Grace.

Things I Wish I Could Have Told You

Don't do it.
I know you think your time is up
That your five minutes of fame was just a fad or phase,
But I still have my snacks and tickets
Nestled in my lap
Ready for your show.
Ready to see your spot-light-*Glee*-inspired moment
Where you shine so bright.
All your friends, family, mentors, and lovers you haven't met yet
Give you a standing ovation—only at intermission
You see, we're only at intermission.
My M&M popcorn concoction is still warm;
My refreshing Sprite is at that perfect stage of condensation
Where the flavor
Is just right—
You are just right.
You don't seem to know it
But there is a crowd counting the moments in your life where you have made us
proud
Where you have blown us away with your talents and expressions—
With who you are.
On stage or not
You have a group of loyal fans who will follow you from your red carpet debut
to your 95th sold-out show
We will be in the first row.
And I am sorry if you don't know
God,
I wish you knew
I am telling you
We have your back—
Understudies at the ready
If the pressure is too much
Bodyguards at your side
If the critics threaten casualties
Chauffeurs in an ally
On standby to whisk you away,
Should the audience get too rowdy
If your hands begin to shake
If the panic sets in
If your voice begins to quake

The way it sometimes does before a performance

We will
Console
You

If your lines don't fit right in your mouth—

Give you the confidence you need in snaps and hollers and between clapping
and shouts,
We will make amphitheaters of our mouths
For you—
Cheering your name
With complete faith
That
You
Are
Everything
You fear you're not.

There is still so much to see. So please,
Take a seat;
Please,

Don't do it.

Mill Creek Canyon

I entered
Another
Earth—
Quiet
Still
And
Untouched
It awakened
Something in me
I hadn't felt
For months.

There among the
Pines & quaking aspens
I felt God
Where He has always
Been—
The summit
Of a mountain—
Mill Creek Canyon.

My bottom
Damp
Left hand
Swollen
And face wet
The leaves shimmied &
Shined
In the afternoon
Light
Like disco sequins

Gracefully
Existing—
Manifesting
His Creation
His original
Design

I wept there

His spirit
Dwelling
In me.

Townhomes on the Marina

Illegal
Immigrant's
Daughter—
I trespass—
A wanderer
Looking for
Refuge
Or
Roots
Only to find
Raw
Timber
Erect
Walls
Framing
&
Studs
Completely
Exposed
Just
Bare bones
Not a graveyard
Of DREAMer's
Aspirations
Just a beginning
Of a home
A beginning
Of hope
The beginning
Of banana bread
Aroma
Cuddling creases
Into the sofa
A navy throw
Knows our bodies
Temperatures
Knows
How you take
The longest road
And hide
your victory points—
This home
Listens
To the rhythm

Of "Archer"
Ringing

Creating
Vibrations
Between
Our breasts
Swaying sweet
Everythings
In each other's ears
Until we
Fall asleep
In one another's
Comfort—

I feel
(somehow)
Less alone

Imagining
This construction site
As my home
I ascend
Unfinished
Plywood stairs
Surmounting
The burnt
Iron nails
And remains
Of men who
Figuratively
&
Literally
Resemble
My father—
Their McDonald's cups & Coke cans
Do not
Litter
This home—
They
Sanctify
It—

I gingerly creep

(aware now
of what I've violated)
to the master
afraid of being
caught between
the beams

(illogical

        but possible)
        Because I remember
        Sheetrock
        Doesn't hold
        In attics
        A lesson I learned
        Tail bone first at
        12 years old
        …
        …no…
        There's no
        Sheetrock here.

        From the corner
        Of the room
        I study the hombre
        Cornflower sky—
        A color which
        Combines my surname
        &
        My heritage
        But doesn't
        Look
        Golden
        Brown
        Like my
                Ancestors
Doesn't
Reflect
Yellow &
Bark materials

…

Trepidation
Encroaches

Like Spaniards

Like smallpox
Like...
Dread
&
I think a thought
I've
Never
Thought...

My mind wants
Placid
Waves
To carry my fears
To the opposite
Shore
        But I let
orange mark lines
snap my anxieties into
place
and I think

Maybe...

        (maybe)

I'm
Meant
To make
Houses
I'll
Never
Live
In...

Maybe
I'm
Foreordained
To erect
Walls to
Keep privilege
In
&
Color
Out.
        ...
Maybe

I am the walls
Maybe I am the splinters
& chips
The nail gun blasting
The "orale wey" y bachata music playing
From my dad's truck
Maybe I am
An outsider

Maybe

A house like this
On Oquirrh Lake
Could
Never
Belong
To a
Trespasser.

I gaze
At the
Refracted

       Light
       Gleaming
       On this
       Sun soaked
       Day
       Shimmering—
       I
       Glide to the kitchen
Now
Bathing
In statistics
I learned in college
In
History
Lessons
&
Slam
Poems
In debates
Some people
Never watch
Or read about
(Or believe)

Because
"everyone has it hard"
I give life to
All the proof
That things are NOT
fair
for an immigrant's daughter
.
..
...

.

.
.
.
.
.
.
.
.
.

.
.
.
.
.
.
.
.
.
.
.
.
.
.
.
.
.
.
.

.
.
and
then

.
..
...

I
Let
It
Go.
Ripples
Drift
All
That
Bullshit
Away

Clenched
Teeth
&
Taut
Clawed
I

Resolve
To change
My legacy
To give opportunity
To make a home
Breathe
My
History
Palpitate
Acceptance
And
Work ethic
Breed
Generosity
&
Love
Throughout
The installation
To wire
A new norm

Where
Every color
Has a home
Like this
Every heritage
Echoes their
Music
In the sheetrock
And
Makes memories
Tender
In finishes
And paint
I pray
We go
Further
I pray for a new
Status quo
To diversify
White enclaves
And
To be the change
I pray every
Wanderer
Or dreamer
So called trespasser
Outsider
Selects their fixtures and
Decorates their futures
In
Every
Conceivable
Aspiration

Making homes
Safe havens.
And statistics
Irrelevant
I pray
Anyone can have a home
Like this—

A home
They built
Themselves.

It is Better to Have Loved

Under the constellations
I recognize truth.
Take note of the luck
And
Chemistry
It took
To get
A night sky so brilliant—
One that only
Occurs
Under seasoned stars,
Time glossed elements,
And human eyes—
In the wonder and awe
Of it all
I recognize
Her.
I see the movement of her hair
Wrapped around a glistening sky.
I see the combusting flecks in her eyes
Reacting to the spotlight of limitless stars.
I see the bursting of love in her lips
Unfolding to create smiles across the canvas of
God's blank space.
In it all
I
See
Her.
A moment of reverence is cast
Over my silhouette soul,
And I know
She's dusted
Constellations
Over my heart—
If for nothing else,
To
Make
Me
Whole.

La Luna

Observing the waxing crescent
I think back to when I was a child—
That iridescent electric glow—
I considered life
Outside of our world
I thought about neighbor boy Alonso and his science teacher telling
him there are literal millions
Of galaxies
"You're telling me, we are the only ones?"
I, perplexed, contrasted this new evidence
To my Catholic Sunday school lessons—
Lukewarm holy water
Making crosses across my forehead
X-ing out my follies.
I gazed at the moon—
Her face a DreamWorks boy's pier,
And I admired
The Alonso boy's certainty—
The imagination of it all.
With sharpened eyes I looked at the dull
Lack of rays
Muted
All
Around,
And I
Stood perplexed again.
Infinite space
Unexplained
In the pages of gilded edged
Leather bound
Holy-scented
Texts.

Of course, now
Glistens of hope
And Kolob
Hymns
Churned with
Paul's third heaven—
Clarify
Infinite space
And
All Alonso's
Rhetorical questions.

Now, of course,
La Luna's
Face appears
A freckle
Of what I know

Of who we are
On the other side of someone else's dream work.

From The Author

This book is a collection of therapy-esq purgings during an extremely difficult period of my life. I hope that every reader can see the progression and movement toward self-love & self-acceptance. Because love wins.

I wrote *RWLU* because I *need* others who are struggling with their sexuality and/or idenity as a member of the Church of Jesus Christ of Latter-Day Saints to understand: you *are* a child of God. You *are* loved by heavenly parents.

Sometimes we get stuck in a cycle of thoughts that seem endless and omnipotent, thoughts like; *nobody understands, I have to choose, what is wrong with me, I'm going to be alone forever, I'd rather be dead.* But those are lies that evil wants you to believe. The world needs your light. Needs your diversity. Needs your spirit. The world is vast! It is much bigger than the narravtives centered in church culture and conformity. There are places you will see and people you will meet that will encircle you in arms of love. Let love win.

In America the second leading cause of death among youth is suicide. Queer youth are almost 5 times more likely than non-queer youth to attempt suicide. Trans youth are almost 6 times more likely to attempt suicide. LGBTQ+ teens who do not have family support/acceptance are 8.4 times more likely to attempt suicide. Sources are listed on the sources page.

We can do better. We can all show love to one another with acts of charity and acceptance.

Choose to stay & choose to love.

-L. Flores

Acknowledgments

There are many people to thank for the help, guidance, support, and love I've recieved while writing *RWLU*. First and foremost I recognize the guidance of Heavenly Parents who know and love me.

I am grateful to my earthly parents for always loving me and consistenly teaching me that anything is possible. All my concievable apsirations will become a reality because they spoke truth to me from the time I was young; *if you can envision it, you can do it*. Thanks mom & dad.

The Duncans who hate slam poetry but love me. Kar, thank you for loving me unconditionally. Thank you for believing in me. Thank you for letting me drag you to slams and *staying*.

The publication of this work wouldn't be possible without the talent and help of Alexis Rashak and Stephen Klopfenstein.

There are many writers who inspire me and I have them to thank as well.

Andrea/Andrew Gibson
Franny Choi
Jeffrey R. Holland
Sarah Kay
Pasely Rekdal
Sierra DeMulder

The poet who most influenced me and began my love of poetry is Emily Dickinson. In homage to her, the greatest female poet to ever live, I wrote "If I were Emily Dickson." Shout-out to 8th period 2019-2020!

If I were Emily Dickinson

I exclaimed
At noonday
                    "I will buy a bike!"
Then suddenly
In unison
There was a swift
Reply
                    "no!"
            Reminiscent of her voice
            Ringing all around
            She made it
            Clear
            She'd leave me sooner
            Should I choose to drive.
When I questioned—
The girls
Sung a similar tune
            "you'll die a horrid Death"
            At this
            I stood
                    Introspectively
            Awaiting my Doom—
                    My own funeral song
            A dirge & eulogy
            Sprays and Casket
            Tombstone
            Inscribed
                    "all she wanted was a bike"
            A Honda
            To
            Be
            Specific!

For all the wanting
            And all the wishing
            Was this image true?

Perhaps the thrill
Was in bloom
Intoxication & ebullience
Speeding in canyons wide,
Fall colors splashing
Euphoria in my eyes.

The feeling of being alive

Was this image true?

...

...

...

Or perhaps

(thinking to myself)

Concealing an
        Insidious inclination
        More than
        Imploring to
        Satisfy
        An accompanying
        Thirst

                —a darker desire—

                —Death,

                        Forevermore.

Sources

CDC, NCIPC. Web-based Injury Statistics Query and Reporting System (WIS QARS) [online]. (2010) {2013 Aug. 1}. Available from:www.cdc.gov/ ncipc/wisqars.

CDC. (2016). Sexual Identity, Sex of Sexual Contacts, and Health-Risk Behaviors Among Students in Grades 9-12: Youth Risk Behavior Surveillance. Atlanta, GA: U.S. Department of Health and Human Services.

James, S. E., Herman, J. L., Rankin, S., Keisling, M., Mottet, L., & Anafi, M. (2016). The Report of the 2015 U.S. Transgender Survey. Washington, DC: National Center for Transgender Equality.

Family Acceptance Project™. (2009). Family rejection as a predictor of negative health outcomes in white and Latino lesbian, gay, and bisexual young adults. Pediatrics. 123(1), 346-52.

CDC. (2016). Sexual Identity, Sex of Sexual Contacts, and Health-Risk Behaviors Among Students in Grades 9-12: Youth Risk Behavior Surveillance. Atlanta, GA: U.S. Department of Health and Human Services.

IMPACT. (2010). Mental health disorders, psychological distress, and suicidality in a diverse sample of lesbian, gay, bisexual, and transgender youths. American Journal of Public Health. 100(12), 2426-32.

More resources @ https://www.thetrevorproject.org/resources/preventing-sui- cide/facts-about-suicide/

"...remember it is by divine design that not all the voices in God's choir are the same."

—Jeffrey R. Holland

Made in the USA
Middletown, DE
09 May 2022

65400690R00040